EARTH SHAPERS
HOW SUPERVOLCANOES
SHAPED EARTH

by Jane P. Gardner

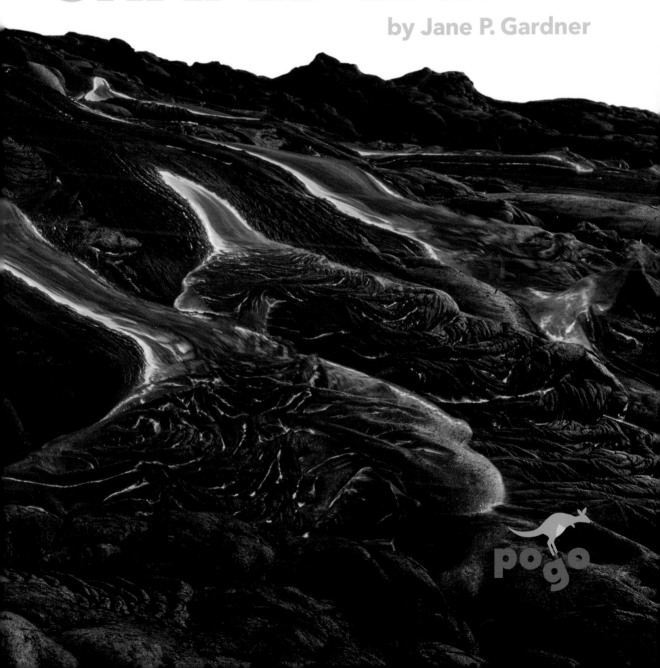

pogo

Ideas for Parents and Teachers

Pogo Books let children practice reading informational text while introducing them to nonfiction features such as headings, labels, sidebars, maps, and diagrams, as well as a table of contents, glossary, and index.

Carefully leveled text with a strong photo match offers early fluent readers the support they need to succeed.

Before Reading

- "Walk" through the book and point out the various nonfiction features. Ask the student what purpose each feature serves.
- Look at the glossary together. Read and discuss the words.

Read the Book

- Have the child read the book independently.
- Invite him or her to list questions that arise from reading.

After Reading

- Discuss the child's questions. Talk about how he or she might find answers to those questions.
- Prompt the child to think more. Ask: The ash and dirt from supervolcanoes can block out the sun and make Earth colder. How do you think life on Earth would change if it was colder?

Pogo Books are published by Jump!
5357 Penn Avenue South
Minneapolis, MN 55419
www.jumplibrary.com

Library of Congress Cataloging-in-Publication Data

Names: Gardner, Jane P., author.
Title: How supervolcanoes shaped Earth / Jane P. Gardner.
Description: Minneapolis, MN: Jump!, Inc., [2021]
Series: Earth shapers | Includes index.
Audience: Ages 7-10.
Identifiers: LCCN 2019028759 (print)
LCCN 2019028760 (ebook)
ISBN 9781645271239 (hardcover)
ISBN 9781645271246 (paperback)
ISBN 9781645271253 (ebook)
Subjects: LCSH: Supervolcanoes—Juvenile literature. Earth sciences—Juvenile literature. | Earth (Planet)—Internal structure—Juvenile literature. | CYAC: Volcanoes.
Classification: LCC QE521.3 .G38 2021 (print)
LCC QE521.3 (ebook) | DDC 551.21—dc23
LC record available at https://lccn.loc.gov/2019028759
LC ebook record available at https://lccn.loc.gov/2019028760

Editor: Jenna Gleisner
Designer: Michelle Sonnek

Photo Credits: Natali Glado/Shutterstock, cover; Yvonne Baur/Shutterstock, 1; Zack Frank/Shutterstock, 3; sydeen/Shutterstock, 4; Mark Garlick/Science Photo Library/Getty, 5; Ralf Lehmann/Shutterstock, 6-7; Pavel Szabo/Shutterstock, 8; LuYago/Shutterstock, 9; Wead/Shutterstock, 10-11; Photovolcanica.com/Shutterstock, 12-13; Jimmy69/iStock, 14-15; Tomas Nevesely/Shutterstock, 16; Susanne Pommer/Shutterstock, 17; JessHatt/Shutterstock, 18-19; Andrey_Popov/Shutterstock, 20-21; Pyty/Shutterstock, 20-21 (screen, top left); JacobH/iStock, 20-21 (screen, top right); stihii/Shutterstock, 20-21 (screen, bottom right); AHMAD FAIZAL YAHYA/Shutterstock, 23.

Printed in the United States of America at Corporate Graphics in North Mankato, Minnesota.

TABLE OF CONTENTS

CHAPTER 1

··

ERUPTION!

This is Lake Toba. It is in Indonesia. This lake was not always here. What formed it?

Lake Toba

A **supervolcano**! It **erupted** more than 70,000 years ago. The volcano collapsed. It created a **depression** called a **caldera**. It filled with water. This is where Lake Toba now sits.

Supervolcanoes are the largest volcanoes. They change the land when they erupt. **Lava** cools. It hardens. It builds up the land.

DID YOU KNOW?

Scientists **rank** eruptions. How? They use a scale. It goes from one to eight. It ranks how much volcanoes spew. Supervolcanoes rank the highest. They are a level eight!

lava

CHAPTER 2

FORMING CALDERAS

So why do supervolcanoes erupt?
And how do calderas form?

caldera

Heat from Earth's **core** melts rock. It melts into **magma**. Magma rises. This builds **pressure**. It pushes up on Earth's **crust**.

magma

The pressure keeps building. The magma must go somewhere. Eruption! It breaks through the crust! After it is above the ground, magma is called lava.

Ash, dust, and dirt fill the air. The **plume** spreads far. It can block out the sun. This makes Earth's surface colder. Plants and animals can die.

DID YOU KNOW?

Supervolcanoes create a lot of ash, dirt, and dust! How much? Scientists think the one under Yellowstone National Park could cover the whole state of Texas with five feet (1.5 meters) of material!

plume

The raised area of ground collapses. Why? The magma that was under it is gone. A large depression forms. This is the caldera.

Earth has many calderas. Phlegraean Fields is one. It is in Italy. It formed almost 40,000 years ago. People now live on top of it.

Phlegraean Fields

TAKE A LOOK!

How do calderas form? Take a look!

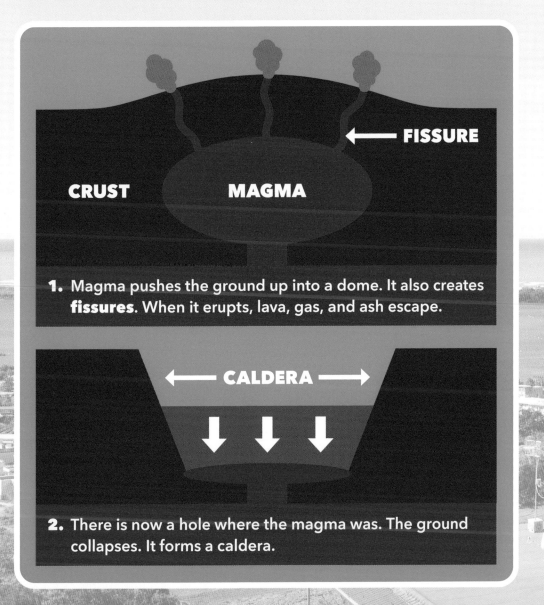

CRUST **MAGMA** **FISSURE**

1. Magma pushes the ground up into a dome. It also creates **fissures**. When it erupts, lava, gas, and ash escape.

CALDERA

2. There is now a hole where the magma was. The ground collapses. It forms a caldera.

CHAPTER 3

SUPERVOLCANOES TODAY

How many supervolcanoes are there? We don't know for sure. But scientists study those we do know about. There is one under Yellowstone National Park. It last erupted more than 640,000 years ago! Magma is close to Earth's surface here. It creates **hot springs**.

Grand Prismatic Spring

Geysers shoot hot water and steam into the air!

Old Faithful Geyser

Lake Taupo

Taupo is a supervolcano in New Zealand. It is the most recent one to erupt. When? It was 22,600 years ago! The caldera filled with water. Lake Taupo now sits here.

DID YOU KNOW?

Taupo created a huge ash plume. How tall was it? Scientists think it rose 31 miles (50 kilometers) high! This is longer than 545 football fields!

Today, some supervolcanoes are **extinct**. Scientists think they will never erupt again. Others are **dormant**. This means they have not erupted in more than 10,000 years. They could erupt one day. But scientists agree. It won't happen for thousands of years.

Supervolcano Analysis

Home   Dashboard   Repoting   Customization   Help   Log Out

Country
City
Status

ACTIVITIES & TOOLS

ASH AND DUST

Huge amounts of ash, dust, and rock erupt from supervolcanoes. See how far heavier and smaller materials move with this activity!

What You Need:
- disposable cup
- plastic wrap
- tape or rubber band
- scissors
- small objects of roughly the same size, such as torn pieces of paper, a cut-up sponge, corks, sand, and flour

1. **Carefully cut a round hole in the bottom of the disposable cup.**

2. **Cover the open end of the cup with plastic wrap. Put tape or a rubber band around the edges to keep it in place.**

3. **Line up the small objects on a counter or table.**

4. **Point the hole in the cup at one of the objects. Gently pull back on the plastic wrap. Release to send a puff of air out of the cup and at the object.**

5. **Repeat with each of the objects. Which materials go farthest? Relate your observations to the material that is erupted out of a supervolcano.**

GLOSSARY

caldera: A large depression formed by the collapse of a volcano or supervolcano after an eruption.

core: The central part of Earth that is very hot.

crust: The hard outer layer of Earth.

depression: A hollow or concave place that curves inward.

dormant: A volcano that is inactive but could become active again.

erupted: To have suddenly and violently thrown lava, hot ash, and steam into the air.

extinct: A volcano that will not erupt again.

fissures: Long, deep, and narrow openings or cracks that occur from breaking or parting.

geysers: Underwater hot springs that shoot boiling water and steam into the air.

hot springs: Sources of hot water that flow naturally from the ground.

lava: The hot, liquid rock that pours out of a volcano when it erupts.

magma: Melted rock beneath Earth's surface that becomes lava when it flows out of volcanoes.

plume: A column of hot volcanic ash and gas that is emitted into the atmosphere after a volcanic eruption.

pressure: The force produced by pressing on something.

rank: To assign a position or level to.

supervolcano: A volcano that erupts at a level eight on the Volcanic Explosivity Index, creating at least 240 cubic miles (1,000 cubic km) of material.

INDEX

TO LEARN MORE

Finding more information is as easy as 1, 2, 3.

1. Go to www.factsurfer.com
2. Enter "howsupervolcanoesshapedEarth" into the search box.
3. Choose your book to see a list of websites.

FACT SURFER